JOHN SUMMERS & SYLVIA CORTHORN

The shocking truth of an Ottawa lawyer and an Ontario Superior Court Judge

Peter Tremblay, ed.

Agora Books™
Ottawa, Canada

John Summers & Sylvia Corthorn: The shocking truth of an Ottawa lawyer and an Ontario Superior Court Judge

© 2021 by Peter Tremblay

All Rights Reserved. No part of this book may be reproduced, stored in a retrieval system, or transmitted in any form or by any means, electronic or mechanical, including photocopying, recording, or otherwise without the expressed written consent of The Agora Cosmopolitan.

Care has been taken to trace ownership / source of any academic or other reference materials contained in this text. The publisher will gratefully accept any information that will enable it to rectify any reference or credit in subsequent edition(s), of any incorrect or omitted reference or credit.

Agora Books
P.O. Box 24191
300 Eagleson Road
Kanata, Ontario K2M 2C3

Agora Books is a self-publishing agency for authors that was launched by The Agora Cosmopolitan which is a registered not-for-profit corporation.

ISBN 978-1-927538-95-1

Printed in Canada

Contents

Introduction..5

Appendix: Recusal Motion against Justice Sylvia Corthorn . . . 15

Introduction

There are many good, ethical judges. But it is apparent that Ontario Justice Sylvia Corthorn is not one of them. It also cannot be said that Mr. John Summers is the most righteous of all lawyers in Canada's capital either. The combined activities of Justice Corthorn and Mr. Summers are responsible for incalculable suffering resulting in the premature death of a black Jewish woman.

On the 24th of May, 2017, Justice Macloed with great integrity implored John Summers to independently verify the well-being and desires of Ms. Dezrin Carby-Samuels. Reportedly, she had been forcibly confined by her husband for years after he had rendered her unable to walk, talk, and write as a result of prolonged domestic abuse.

Mr. Summers was contacted by his "handlers" who arranged for the replacement of Justice Macloed with Justice Corthorn, who seized the case to prevent ethical judges like Justice Macloed from seeking to save Ms. Carby-Samuels' life.

Having witnessed a variety of irregularities suggesting profound corruption and racism by Justice Corthorn, the son of Ms.

Carby-Samuels, who sought to rescue his mother from domestic violence perpetrated by Mr. Summers, decided to pursue the recusal of Justice Corthorn based upon a tip from a whistleblower at the Ottawa courthouse who was privy to the illicit actions of Justice Corthorn and Mr. Summers (*See* Appendix).

Justice Corthorn became alarmed that "her work" on behalf of rogue elements was in jeopardy. Evidence of irregularities by Judge Corthorn were so extensive that Ontario Superior Court Administrative Justice Beaudoin approved the recusal motion requested by Ms. Carby-Samuels's son.

The son of Ms. Carby-Samuels was a plaintiff in the case after having been forced to sue Ms. Carby-Samuels's husband, who blocked the son's access to his mom after the son reported seeing the husband physically assault his mother and engage in other forms of domestic abuse.

Having been inserted in the trial, Justice Corthorn did what any self-respecting dirty judge would be expected to do. She pretended that no motion to remove her from the case existed and allowed John Summers to fabricate a motion unlawfully signed by Ms. Georgette Cleroux, her own secretary, who had no legal standing in the case. The motion was then used to declare the son of Ms. Carby-Samuels a "vexatious litigant" for seeking to save his mother's life from the "medical experiment" that rogue elements had sought to perpetuate against Ms. Carby-Samuels and her apparently mind-controlled husband, who seems to have been programmed to perpetrate domestic violence. Justice Corthorn then expedited a "Summary Judgement" on behalf of Mr. Summers in an effort to further frustrate Judge Beaudoin's efforts to get her kicked off the case.

By declaring "Summary Judgement," Judge Corthorn sought to thwart any further judicial inquiry of her quasi-criminal conduct, which includes evidence of collusion with Mr. Summers. Judge Corthorn presided over a rigged kangaroo court for the explicit purpose of perpetuating human torture, which resulted in Ms. Carby-Samuels not being able to walk, talk and write. Then, having lost all independent mobility, Ms. Carby-Samuels was forced to suffer and waste away into a terrible death while being unable to see her son as a result of a criminal conspiracy of epic proportions.

Officially, Mr. Summers was the lawyer of Mr. Carby-Samuels. But Mr. Summers was recorded having admitted to the son of Ms. Carby-Samuels that this was a complete ruse and that he "was not at liberty to say" who was paying him as his effective client.

Mr. Carby-Samuels was subjected to a sort of mind-controlled state that could be used to perpetuate torture of his wife, and it was the apparent mission of Mr. Summers and Ms. Corthorn to thwart any efforts by ethical judges and the son of Ms. Carby-Samuels to help make his mother better and to liberate her from this evil plot.

You might rightfully think that all this business of "mind control" is just outrageous. But there is a well-established paper trail of mind-control-related experiments that have surfaced from time to time, which include the infamous "Montreal Experiments" of the late 1950s and early 1960s. It appears that somehow Mr. Carby-Samuels was the target of an experiment to remove his consciousness from his body and then to replace it with a complete psychopath who then began to beat and torture Ms. Carby-Samuels. The most telling evidence of this process was the fact that after this "substitution process" was complete, Mr. Carby-Samuels's signature radically changed from a precise signature he had maintained for over 60 years.

Justice Corthorn's role in all of this was through "Summary Judgement" to cover up the testimony of multiple handwriting experts, who all affirmed in an affidavit that in their expert representation that the signature collected by Mr. John Summers from Horace Carby-Samuels and the verifiable signatures of Horace Carby-Samuels could not be the same people.

The son of Dezrin Carby-Samuels began to suspect a broader agenda when Horace Carby-Samuels began to express paranoia about an "Extraterrestrial threat." It appears that Horace Carby-Samuels began to perceive the efforts to remove his consciousness from his body and to replace it with a different one as a manipulative alien operation.

It was Justice Patrick Smith who in February 2016 rendered a default judgement in favour of the son of Ms. Carby-Samuels. That judgement ruled that the son ought to have daily access to Ms. Carby-Samuels in order to ensure the well-being of his mother.

The backroom criminals who sought to target both Dezrin and Horace Carby-Samuels did not like this judgement and wanted Dezrin (and Horace) for themselves. So, in March 2016, they inserted John Summers to ensure Dezrin Carby-Samuels's misery would be perpetuated under the "lock and key" of her husband who had been mind-controlled into a psychopath to torture his wife.

John Summers's role in the premature death of Dezrin Carby-Samuels is further documented in the book entitled *John*

Summers: The Untold Story of Corruption, Systemic Racism and Evil at Bell Baker LLP.

With that said, perhaps the biggest question in all this is how did a dedicated mother and retired registered nurse who has never had a political agenda in her life become the target of a well-organized and well-financed group of backroom criminals aided and abetted by a lawyer and, much more shockingly, a judge?

It is apparent that Ms. Dezrin Carby-Samuels and her husband Horace Carby-Samuels were chosen by these group of backroom criminals for heinous medical experiment involving mind control, abuse, and gaslighting. These criminals then inserted John Summers to concoct a fictitious defence supported by equally fictitious motions designed to prevent at all costs the son of Ms. Dezrin Carby-Samuels and Horace Carby-Samuels from saving them from the "progress" of these experiments. These experiments began under the auspices of Dr. Jerry T.

It became apparent to the son of Dezrin Carby-Samuels that his mom was being subjected to bizarre medical experiments after he saw reviews about this doctor who developed quite a reputation online for guinea pig experiments that drew the anger of his former patients who managed to escape with their lives. These patients online remarked how they quickly got better after they stopped seeing Dr. J.

That's when the son of Dezrin Carby-Samuels knew that if only he could free his mother from the control from this doctor, she would be able to enjoy a similar speedy recovery from guinea pig experiments.

Thanks to these experiments, Ms. Carby-Samuels was transformed from a very healthy and arguably super, woman at her age who expected to live as long as her grandmother who lived to about 104, to a completely crippled and destroyed woman left to rot in her own fecal matter, who is now in a Jewish cemetery in Ottawa, Canada.

The name of the group that John Summers had confessed to the son of Ms. Carby-Samuels was paying him $300/hr is unknown, but their tactics are self-evident.

Nazi Germany not only had sought to exterminate Jewish people and other minorities. This evil empire had also sought to conduct horrific medical experiments alongside an extermination program.

When Nazi Germany supposedly surrendered to the allies, it is a well-known fact that the same scientists who conducted grotesque experiments on human lives were recruited by backroom criminals who sought to continue those experiments on unsuspecting targeted groups, including vulnerable populations like senior citizens, homeless people, and powerless minority communities.

The "Montreal Experiments" are perhaps the most official and public example of the continuation of Nazi experiments.

The execution of the orchestrated plot involving an Ottawa lawyer and an Ontario Superior Court Judge was reminiscent of Jon Bokenkamp's *Blacklist*, which presents a world run by factions of criminals who run governments and large corporations through an overseeing clique.

Such background criminals bankroll and groom certain people for positions of authority, and when they eventually obtain desired positions of authority, these "Archons" then begin to demand favours that may from time to time include the use of vulnerable individuals and minority communities for medical experiments. These experiments are sheltered from legal scrutiny by the strategically recruited operatives.

Blacklist was apparently so close to the truth that even though it was filmed in 2013 it included an episode in which germ warfare experiment would be released from a laboratory in China that would start a pandemic and that a Chinese scientist whistleblower would seek refuge in the United States alleging that the pandemic plot was the result of genetic engineering. In the *Blacklist* version, the Americans used information from the Chinese whistleblower whom they helped escape from China to completely stop the pandemic.

In 2020, such a whistleblower, whose name is Dr Li-Meng Yan, who also resembled the Chinese scientist in *Blacklist,* made the same allegation. But this time, the world did not listen as in the world depicted in *Blacklist*.

There's an old saying: "Those who ignore the lessons of history are doomed to repeat it."

It was Dr. Michael Salla who also once remarked that "science fiction hides truth in plain sight."

It may be vital that we, as humans, begin to learn the lessons of history and look for the truth that hides in plain sight before us in the critical effort to save our world from the criminal masterminds who are responsible for continued invasive experiments against humans for self-serving evil agendas.

Dezrin Carby-Samuels has become the latest black and Jewish victim of crimes against humanity by those who seek to subvert the rule of law through the manipulation of judges, lawyers, the police, religious leaders, corporate executives, and politicians.

The Pagan Gnostics referred to the group that apparently controls at least one lawyer and Ontario Superior Court judge as the Archons, or, more precisely, the "humanized face of the manipulative aliens" as presented in the extensive research of John Lash on Metahistory.org.

Corthorn J. and John Summers were inserted into the lives of a black Jewish family in behalf of a demonic "fifth column," and as long as the money tap flowed and their job security was ensured by whoever they reported to, they did not have a care in the world as to the human suffering, including torture, which was the result of their nefarious activities.

"Black Lives Matter" has become a slogan which has emerged out of the killing of innocent black people at the hands of operatives who officially are members of police forces. It is apparent that black lives did not matter to Corthorn J. and John Summers and the other operatives named in the book entitled *John Summers: The Untold Story of Corruption, Systemic Racism and Evil at Bell Baker LLP*, all of whom have verifiable ties to each other as that book elaborates.

An Ontario judge and a lawyer using their authority conferred by Her Majesty the Queen of Canada to act as accomplices to the evil plot that was recognized by administrative Justice Beaudoin as being legitimate represents a shocking betrayal of their oaths of office.

This book contains the very motion approved for review by Justice Beaudoin but which Corthorn J. pretended did not exist (*See* Appendix).

It is the respectful opinion of the author of this book that Madame Justice Corthorn has no business presiding over any courtroom that purports to be lawful, and Mr. Summers has no business to practice law in the province of Ontario. The role of Corthorn J and Mr. Summers in the premature death of a black Jewish woman as a result of the nefarious activities associated with the motion that follows requires either their resignation or removal by Crown prosecutors in affirmation of the integrity of the constitutional basis of Canadian laws.

Appendix

Recusal Motion against Justice Sylvia Corthorn

| Search results | Archive | Collapse | Delete | Spam |

OFFICIAL LEGAL NOTICE / DEMAND LETTER - ... (5)

| cosmopolita cosmopolita | Dear Ontario Supe | Oct 5 at 10:10 AM |
| cosmopolita cosmopolita | Corrected letter - r | Oct 5 at 10:17 AM |

Johansson, Tina (JUD) <TinaJohanson@ontario.ca>   Oct 5 at 12:34 PM
To cosmopolita cosmopolita, Creswell, Leslie (JUD)
CC John Summers, Gorette Cleroux

Johanson, Tina (JUD)
✉ TinaJohanson@ontario...
🔍 Search emails

...

+ 3 more contacts

Good afternoon,

I have your email message of October 5, 2017. The method by which to request that a judge consider recusing himself or herself from a matter is not by way of email or letter communication. To obtain an order from a judge recusing himself or herself, you are required to bring a motion. The motion must be before the judge whom you are asking to recuse themselves – in this case, Justice Corthorn. The motion must be supported by an evidentiary record.

Therefore, if it is your intention to request Justice Corthorn to recuse herself, you are required to serve and file the appropriate motion record. Service is required on all parties to the matter or matters for which you are requesting that Justice Corthorn recuse herself.

Please note that further correspondence to me or Ms. Creswell on this issue would be inappropriate. You are required to deal with the civil counter on the matter.

Sincerely,

Tina Johanson

SCJ Trial Coordinator / Coordonnatrice des procès de la CSJ
Criminal and Civil Divisions / affaires criminelles et civiles
Tina.Johanson@ontario.ca

> Show original message

← Reply   ← Reply to All   → Forward   ... More

| cosmopolita cosmopolita | Dear Tina, Thanks | Oct 5 at 1:06 PM |
| Johanson, Tina (JUD) | Mr. Carby-Samuels, The | Oct 5 at 2:12 PM |

Click to Reply, Reply All or Forward

FILE NUMBER: 15-667

ONTARIO

SUPERIOR COURT OF JUSTICE

BETWEEN

RAYMOND CARBY-SAMUELS

Plaintiff

– and –

HORACE R CARBY-SAMUELS

Defendai

AFFIDAVIT OF RAYMOND CARBY-SAMUELS

I, of the City of Ottawa in the Province of Ontario, MAKE OATH AND SAY (or AFFIRM):

1. I, Raymond Carby-Samuels, confirm and attest to the fact that I have a reasonable apprehension of bias regarding the expressed ability of Justice Sylvia Corthorn to preside over the fair and impartial administration of justice as outlined by the Canadian Judicial Council's Code of Ethics.
2. I submit this Motion seeking the immediate and if possible retroactive recusal of Justice Sylvia Corthorn on all matters related to the Defence Counsel's Motions for Summary Judgement and Vexatious Litigant, and ar

other matter related to Court File 15-66772 based upon the legal advisement of Tina Johanson, SCJ Trial Coordinator, Criminal and Civil Divisions of the Superior Court of Justice in Ottawa. [Exhibit 1]

3. I made a complaint to the Canadian Judicial Council dated 6 October 2017 outlining grounds for Justice Sylvia Corthorn's immediate recusal from Court File 15-66772. [Exhibit 2]

4. DISCRIMINATION - Justice Corthorn subjected me to *prima facie* discrimination involving differential treatment as defined by the *Ontario Human Rights Code* by fabricating a "Leave for Urgent Motion" process that is not authorized by the *Ontario Rules of Civil Procedure*; has no apparent legal precedent in common law and gave the appearance of handicapping my efforts pursue my Motion as a self-represented litigant.

5. INSTITUTIONALIZED RACISM / DISCRIMNATION – Whereas Justice Macloed on 24 March 2017 sought to endorse his sought independent verification of my Mom's well-being to ensure that my Mom has not been held "prisoner" to borrow his words, Justice Corthorn expressed no such interest in verifying the safety and security of my Mom, as a black woman, pursuant to the *Canadian Charter of Rights and Freedoms* and have the appearance of racism. Justice Corthorn apparent lack of demonstrated concern for the factual verification of my Mom's well-being and desires that is incumbent of any Judge that seeks to uphold our Constitution requires her immediate recusal. Furthermore, Justice Corthorn gave no regard to the physical disabilities of my Mom in being able to present herself in the Courtroom in violation of Equality Rights stipulated in Section 15(1) of the *Canadian Charter of Rights and Freedoms* while ignoring my presented written evidence of my Mom's desires in lieu of her attendance.

6. APPARENT PREJUDICE IN FAVOUR OF DEFENCE. Justice Sylvia Corthorn on multiple occasions demonstrated apparent bias. This included allowing the Defence to submit documents late in respect of the *Ontario Rules of Civil Procedure* which is based upon supporting a fair litigation process. While Justice Corthorn allowed Defence Counsel to submit late documents, in Justice Corthorn's ruling on the Leave for Urgent Motion, she scolded the Plaintiff who is a self-represented litigant for having made a late submission as a result of the tardiness of the Plaintiff's lawyer who he had no control over. Justice Corthorn also accepted the veracity of claims made by

Defence Counsel regarding the wishes of the Plaintiff's Mom as being the same as the Defendant when she referred to "my parents" in No 11 of her so-called Leave for Urgent Motion ruling even though the Defence Counsel had refused to independently verify the well-being and desires of my Mom. Justice Corthorn therefore has demonstrated a penchant to rule in favour of Defence Counsel without any basis of facts / evidence while disregarding my evidence regarding the stated desires of my Mom.

7. ACCEPTANCE OF APPARENT FAKE SIGNATURE – I have observed by meticulous consistence of my father's signature over the years. Justice Corthorn accepted an affidavit during the Leave for Urgent Motion which was not only late; and contained false information but also contained a signature which in no way resembled signatures by the Defendant that have been consistent in previous Affidavits of the Defendant.

8. KNOWINGLY ACCEPTING FRAUDULENT REPRESENTATION IN AN AFFIDAVIT – Justice Corthon has accepted affidavits knowingly with false information proving a willingness to use this false information to support an Endorsement that has been subjected to prejudice. Examples of Justice Corthorn knowingly accepting Defence Counsel's false information to prejudice the Plaintiff include the Defence Affidavits references to "my parents" not wanting to see or have contact with me when she knew that the Defendant rejected Judge Macloed's sought independent verification; and the Defendant's Affidavit fraudulently alleging that I had been "blacklisted" by Ottawa Ambulance Services even though I presented official correspondence from Ottawa Ambulance Services denying such a "blacklisting". Furthermore, even though Defence Counsel has claimed that the Defendant wants to have no contact with the Plaintiff, Justice Corthorn ignored evidence presented by the Plaintiff that the Defendant actually called the Plaintiff on 21 August 2017 and talked for over two minutes. This is clear proof that Defence Counsel's representation concerning the alleged desire of the Defendant not to have contact as being fraudulent. [Exhibit 2]

9. THE ACCEPTANCE OF INADMISSIBLE AFFIDAVITS submitted by Defence Counsel in support of their Motions for Summary Judgement and Vexatious Litigation. Justice Corthorn has shown a lack of respect for me as a self-represented litigant pursuant to Section 24 of the *Canadian Charter of Rights and Freedoms* by allowing Defence Council to run amok of

established practices of proper Affidavits in relation to the *Ontario Rules of Civil Procedure*. This includes Justice Corthorn allowing Defence Counsel to submit an affidavit by Gorette Cleroux who works for John Summers whose testimony is based upon heresay she skimmed online. At the same time, Justice Corthorn has allowed Defence Council to unilaterally block my own *bona fide* affidavit submissions.

10. DENIAL OF MY RIGHT TO LEGAL REPRESENTATION – My lawyer had sought to seek an adjournment of the Motions for Summary Judgement of Vexatious Litigation to allow him time to prepare since he had take so much time to prepare the Urgent Motion. Justice Corthorn denied my lawyer's request and then forced me to defend myself against Motions for Summary Judgement and Vexatious Litigation against a lawyer who apparently was accepted to the Bar in 1999.

Affirmed before me at the City of Ottawa in the Province of Ontario on _____ OCT 1 0 2017 _____

_____
Commissioner for Taking Affidavits

_____
(Signature of deponent)

← Search results ← ≪ → 🗄 Archive ⊟ Collapse 🗑 Delete ⚑ Sp

OFFICIAL LEGAL NOTICE / DEMAND LETTER - ... (5)

| cosmopolita cosmopolita | Dear Ontario Supe | Oct 5 at 10:10 AM |
| cosmopolita cosmopolita | Corrected letter - r | Oct 5 at 10:17 AM |

Johanson, Tina (JUD) <TinaJohanson@ontario.ca>   Oct 5 at 12:34 PM
To cosmopolita cosmopolita, Creswell, Leslie (JUD)
CC John Summers, Gorette Cleroux

Johanson, Tina (JUD)
✉ TinaJohanson@ontario...
🔍 Search emails

...

+ 3 more contacts

Good afternoon,

I have your email message of October 5, 2017. The method by which to request that a judge consider recusing himself or herself from a matter is not by way of email or letter communication. To obtain an order from a judge recusing himself or herself, you are required to bring a motion. The motion must be before the judge whom you are asking to recuse themselves – in this case, Justice Corthorn. The motion must be supported by an evidentiary record.

Therefore, if it is your intention to request Justice Corthorn to recuse herself, you are required to serve and file the appropriate motion record. Service is required on all parties to the matter or matters for which you are requesting that Justice Corthorn recuse herself.

Please note that further correspondence to me or Ms. Creswell on this issue would be inappropriate. You are required to deal with the civil counter on the matter.

Sincerely,

Tina Johanson

SCJ Trial Coordinator / Coordonnatrice des procès de la CSJ
Criminal and Civil Divisions / affaires criminelles et civiles
TinaJohanson@ontario.ca

> Show original message

← Reply ≪ Reply to All → Forward ••• More

| cosmopolita cosmopolita | Dear Tina, Thanks | Oct 5 at 1:06 PM |
| Johanson, Tina (JUD) | Mr. Carby-Samuels, The | Oct 5 at 2:12 PM |

Court File: 15-66772

B.P 24191 – 300 Eagleson Rd
Kanata, Ontario K2M 2C3

6 October 2017

Canadian Judicial Council,
Ottawa, Ontario, K1A 0W8

Complaint Against Justice Sylvia Corthorn

Dear Canadian Judicial Council representative,

I very respectfully submit a complaint to your Office regarding apparent judicial misconduct and breaches in violation of the *Canadian Judicial Council's Code of Ethics*.

I'm requesting a full investigation of Justice Corthon's treatment of my Court Claim since Her Honour had seized my Claim without my voluntary consent.

I'm hoping that Justice Sylvia Corthorn will voluntarily recuse herself from presiding any further on my Court File 15-66772 on the Ontario Superior Court of Justice in matters specifically relating to my sought Urgent Motion to visit my elderly and sick mother and in general matters related prevailing Defence Motions.

Justice Sylvia Corthorn has totally disregarded the prior endorsement of Justice Macloed who sought independent verification to borrow His Honour's words that my Mother "is not being held prisoner" by my father. [Exhibit 1 – attached]

In doing so, Justice Corthorn to-date has acted in callous disregard of my Mom's life, and in general, the rights of the physically disabled and the plight of women suffering from spousal abuse and human decency along with my own civil rights.

Justice Corthorn for months has perpetuated the abuse of my Mom that she has been subjected to by my father in addition to the subversion of my own rights.

Evidence that I submitted to Justice Corthorn regarding abuse and neglect involving enforced social isolation and deprivation of access to medical care by the Defendant that my Mom had sought to protect her health have been of no apparent concern to this Judge. This blocking of access to medical care has involved the
depriving of speech therapy which resulted in my Mom losing the ability to talk.

Justice Corthorn has denied my Mom her civil rights prescribed in Section 7 regarding "Life, liberty and the security of person" by showing total disregard to my Mom's complaints of abuse and my efforts to establish contact with my Mom, which Her Honour has no basis in law to frustrate, in violation of my freedom of conscience and religion as affirmed in the *Canadian Charter of Rights and Freedoms*.

In Justice Corthon's decision [no 11], she referred to what "my parents" want in relationship to my Mother when she has no basis of fact to be making this reference.

The Defendant denied Justice's MacLoed stated endorsement in the transcript attached of my 24 March 2017 Motion to support a process of independent verification to ensure to borrow His Honour's words that my Mom is "not being held prisoner".

It is therefore a categorical demonstration of prejudice and bias for Justice Corthorn to then make a claim of what "my parents" [i.e. cited in no 11 of her Ruling -- Exhibit 2] want solely based on the veracity of Defendant's heresay claims in his affidavit that he has sought to block independent verification.

Justice Corthon has shown in Her Honour's ruling that unlike Justice Macloed, she will not be guided by evidence and facts. Instead, Justice Corthorn has shown a prejudicial bias in support of / in favour of any and all claims of the Defendant irrespective of any evidence to the contrary.

I have presented evidence to Justice Corthorn that my Mom has maintained a desire to see me. But instead, Justice Corthorn has made misleading statements regarding the desires of my Mom without any basis of fact or evidence.

There is no greater responsibility entrusted to Judges across Canada under our *Canadian Charter of Rights and Freedoms* that the protection of life.

The Supreme Court of Canada has affirmed that judges are required to use their inherent jurisdiction to affirm the protection of life and especially in matters regarding children and the physically disabled like my Mom; and Justice Corthorn has failed miserably in her Oath to Her Majesty which is implicitly based on this axiom.

Furthermore, Justice Corthorn elected to base her decision on an Affidavit submitted by Defence Counsel that was late in violation of the *Ontario Rules of Civil Procedure*, contained verifiable slander alleging that I had been "blacklisted" by the Ottawa Ambulance Services" [Exhibit 4] and according to my Handwriting experts, the signed Affidavit was subject to forgery. [Exhibit 3].

In her ruling, Justice Corthorn sought to chastise the lateness of my lawyer who had been preparing the Urgent Motion but failed to similar chastise the repeated lateness of Defence Counsel in violation of Civil Procedure which further shows bias.

I would also add that Justice Corthorn has subjected me to differential treatment in violation of the Ontario Human Rights Code by requiring that my Urgent Motion be submitted first through a "Leave of Urgent Motion" to Her Honour. There's no such thing in the Ontario Rules of Civil Procedure as a "Leave of Urgent Motion" which she contrived in violation of my civil rights and supports a reasonable apprehension of bias

I hope that Justice Corthorn will do the Honorable thing and immediately recuse herself from having subjected me to bias and prejudice in her Courtroom and for having perpetuated the abuse of my Mother which had resulted in my reasonable apprehension of bias against her ability to treat my file based upon actual evidence and facts, and to affirm my desire for equity pursuant to Section 96 of the Courts of Justice Act

Thanks for your consideration.

Kind regards,

Raymond Carby-Samuels

cc. Office of Justice Corthorn

Offices of MacNamara, JS

EXPERT AFFIDAVIT OF GRACIE CARR

STATE OF NEW YORK

COUNTY OF BROOME

BE IT KNOWN, that on this 10th day of September 2017.

BEFORE ME, a duly sworn and competent authority in and for the County of Broome, NOTARY PUBLIC, and the undersigned affiant and competent witness appearing herein below,

DID PERSONALLY APPEAR: GRACE CARR, a person of fully age of Majority, residing and domiciled in the State of New York, County of Broome.

WHO AFTER BEEN DULY SWORN BY ME, did depose and state:

(1) My name is Dr Grace Carr and I have personal knowledge of the matters contained in this Affidavit. I am a licensed and practicing Forensic Expert in detecting forged signature in the State of New York. I have been practicing as a Forensic Expert for 10 years. I am over the age of eighteen years, am of sound mind, having never been convicted of a felony or a crime of moral turpitude; I am competent in all respect to make this declaration. I have personal knowledge of the matters herein.

(2) I have studied, trained and hold a certification in the examination, comparison, analysis and identification of Signatures from The International School of Forensic Document Examination. I have served as an expert within pending litigation matters.

(3) I was asked to compare the signature on Exhibit A, Exhibit B and Exhibit C. After carefully examining and analyzing the signature in Exhibit A, Exhibit B and Exhibit C. It is my opinion that the signatures of Mr. Horace Carby-Samuels in three different documentation are resulted from three different timelines.

(4) In the first documentation is Court File no. 1771624 which seems to hold the original signature of Mr. Horace Carby-Samuels (exhibit A) Similarly in the second documentation, Court File no.15-66772 (exhibit B) which has the alleged false signature along with the third documentation with the same Court File no. 15-66772(exhibit C) which has been used as preference for additional clarity.

(5) From the basic analysis, the first and third documents are signed by the same individual however; it seems to be clear that the second documentation has a forged signature .According to the formal analysis this type of forgery of signature would be classified as the simulated signature, or "free hand forgery" as it is sometime known. This forgery is constructed by using a genuine signature as a model. The forger generates an artistic reproduction of this model. Depending on his skill and amount of practice, the simulation may be quite good and bear remarkable pictorial similarity to the genuine signature.

(6) Many simulations created with a model at hand will contain at least some of the general indicators of forgery, such as tremor, hesitation, pen lifts, blunt starts and stops, patching, and static pressure. They will have a slow "drawn" appearance. The practiced simulation is most often a higher quality creation in that the model signature has been memorized and some of the movements used to produce it have become semi-automatic. This simulation can be written with a more natural fluid manner. There can be tapered starts and stops, changes in pen pressure, and much less tremor in the moving line. Speed lends fluidity to writing. The more rapidly the pen moves while creating the genuine writing or signature, the more difficult the genuine writing is to imitate. Rapidly formed movements are scrutinized more closely than slower counterparts. A slowly written signature is not only easier for the forger to duplicate with some fashionable degree of pictorial similarity; the product will also display indications of non-genuineness than the forgery of a rapid and fluidly executed signature. The writer of a simulation must, of necessity, pay more attention to the form of a letter than the speed of his pen.

(7) Both practiced and non-practiced simulations will still have notable shortcomings. The forger naturally puts his greatest effort into those parts of the name that he expects to fall under the greatest scrutiny. Although letter forms (especially the more prominent, large or beginning letters) may almost duplicate the genuine letters, proportions and height ratios will seldom be correct. Internal portions of the names (smaller, less prominent letters and pen movements) will usually display the greatest divergence from the correct form and movements found in the genuine signature. During the creation of a simulated forgery, the author attempts to duplicate the writing style of another individual. By doing this, the forger leaves behind little, if any, of his own distinctive writing style. By doing an emulation of someone else's signature, he also produces one of the best of all possible disguises of his own handwriting. Infrequently, some of the forger's own individual characteristics may appear in the disputed writing. The limited quantity of these characteristics which appear on those occasions is such that identification of the author almost never occurs. If there are a sufficient number of significant differences between the questioned signature and the genuine signatures, and these same differences appear in the practiced simulations, there may be a basis to associate the forgery to the forger within some degree of probability. An absolute identification, nonetheless, even under these circumstances is infrequent.

(8) Closely related to this form of identification process is that of determining the number of different forgers from a quantity of simulations. On occasion there will be two or more forgers attempting to reproduce the same signature. It may be possible to group or associate simulations of the same name by the combinations of defects within the forgeries. By associating and grouping the similar defects (when compared to the genuine signature) it may be possible to conclude and illustrate that there are indeed, two or more different forgers.

(9) The second documentation (Exhibit 2) clearly projects the forged signature for the following reasoning

In the second document it can identified that the forger places the pen point in contact with the paper, and then starts writing. When he or she is finished with the name or some portion thereof, he or she stops the pen and lifts it from the surface. This has cause the emphasized blunt start and ending where the pen was placed in contact with the surface. At times this contact is held so long that the pen contains two fluid inks in the front letter of the signature, it has wet the paper and migrate outward from the contact point.

There may be unnecessary and extraneous marks caused by pen starts and stops. The writer may decided after putting his or her pen in contact with the paper, that it is in the wrong spot, picks it up and moves it to a position considered more correct. Normally a signature's starts and stops are much more dynamic which can be noticed in the other two documents. The pen is moving horizontally before it contacts the paper and is lifted at the end while still in flight. This leaves a tapered appearance at the beginnings and endings of names or letters.

In this situation it can occasioned that the pen stops at an unusual point in the writing; perhaps during radical change in direction is about to take a new letter formation is about to be started. This may take on the appearance of a larger gap in the written line where one is not expected, or an overlapping of two ink lines where there should be only one continuous line which clearly in the second document but not the other two, where it seems to be following the same pattern throughout the signature.

Because the creation of most forms of non-genuine signatures are little more than drawings, the pen is moving so slowly that small, sometimes microscopic changes in direction take place in what should be a fluid-looking line. The resultant line is not smooth, but reflects the "shaking" pen. It can be seen that the lines in the signature of the second documentation is much larger than the rest two and has microscopic shakes.

Again, because the pen is moving slowly rather than with the dynamic movement associated with most genuine writings, the ink line remains constant in thickness, resulting from the same constant pressure exerted on a slowly moving pen. There will be little, if any, tapering of internal lines. This is clearly evident in the second document's signature which constantly remains in the same thickness.

Sometimes when the genuine writer makes an error while writing our own signature, more commonly individuals may leave the signature alone, caring little about the mistake or imperfection, while others will simply "fix" the signature by correcting the offending portion. This might have been done in this situation to make the signature more readable, or because a defect in the pen or paper has affected what we perceive to be our "normal" signature, or for some other reason that may even be subconscious.

However by analyzing the previous signature that seems very unlikely. These "fixes" are patent, with no attempt made on the part of the writer to mask or otherwise hide the correction for which some letters are crossing the others out.

These signature corrections are quite different than the patching that is frequently found in non-genuine signatures. On these occasions, the writer is not attempting to make the signature more readable, but to make its appearance passable. He or she is fixing an obvious defect that he or she perceives as detectable, and might uncover his fraudulent product and foil his scheme. These usually take the form of a correction to a flaw in the writing line rather than in the form of a letter. Extensions to entry or terminal strokes, or to lower descending portions of letters, along with corrections to embellishments, are typical of non-genuine patching.

It is my professional opinion that the documentation in (exhibit B) has a forged signature of Mr. Horace R. Carby-Samuels and with intent of malicious actions.

Dated: September 10, 2017

I affirm the truth of this statement

GRACE CARR

STATE OF NEW YORK
COUNTY OF BROOME

I, the undersigned Notary Public, in and for the said State and County, hereby certify that Dr Grace Carr whose name is signed to the foregoing Affidavit, and who is known to me, acknowledged before me on this day that, being informed of said Affidavit, He executed same voluntarily on the day the same bears date.

Given under my hand and seal this 10th day of September, 2017

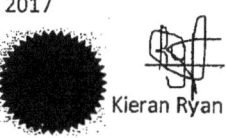

Kieran Ryan

Notary Public

To: The Ontario Supreme Court of Justice

From:

Date: September 16th 2017

Re: Horace R. Carby-Samuels v. Raymond Carby-Samuels, Court file no. 17-71624, Court file no. 1566772

ISSUE

Mr. Raymond Carby Samuels has brought forward the following documents in Exhibit A, Exhibit B and Exhibit C for investigation in the claims of forgery of the signatures of Mr. Horace R.Carby-Samuels.

From handwriting experts reports it has been analysed the signature of Mr. Horace Carby-Samuels in three different documentation are resulted from three different timelines.

In the first documentation is Court File no. 1771624 which seems to hold the original signature of Mr Horace Carby-Samuels (exhibit A)

Similarly in the second documentation, Court File no.15-66772 (exhibit B) which has the alleged false signature along with the third documentation with the same Court File no. 15-66772(exhibit C) which has been used as preference for additional clarity.

From the basic analysis, the first and third documents are signed by the same individual however; it seems to be clear that the second documentation has a forged signature.

BRIEF ANSWER

According to the formal analysis this type of forgery of signature would be classified as the simulated signature, or "free hand forgery" as it is sometime known. This forgery is constructed by using a genuine signature as a model. The forger generates an artistic reproduction of this model. Depending on his skill and amount of practice, the simulation may be quite good and bear remarkable pictorial similarity to the genuine signature.

Many simulations created with a model at hand will contain at least some of the general indicators of forgery, such as tremor, hesitation, pen lifts, blunt starts and stops, patching, and static pressure. They will have a slow "drawn" appearance. The practiced simulation is most often a higher quality creation in that the model signature has been memorized and some of the movements used to produce it have become semi-automatic. This simulation can be written with a more natural fluid manner. There can be tapered starts and stops, changes in pen pressure, and much less tremor in the moving line. Speed lends fluidity to writing. The more rapidly the pen moves while creating the genuine writing or signature, the more difficult the genuine writing is to imitate. Rapidly formed movements are scrutinized more closely than slower counterparts. A slowly written signature is not only easier for the forger to duplicate with some fashionable degree of pictorial similarity; the product will also display indications of non-genuineness than the forgery of a rapid and fluidly executed signature. The writer of a simulation must, of necessity, pay more attention to the form of a letter than the speed of his pen.

Both' practiced and non-practiced simulations will still have notable shortcomings. The forger naturally puts his greatest effort into those parts of the name that he expects to fall under the greatest scrutiny. Although letter forms (especially the more prominent, large or beginning letters) may almost duplicate the genuine letters, proportions and height ratios will seldom be correct. Internal portions of the names (smaller, less prominent letters and pen movements) will usually display the greatest divergence from the correct form and movements found in the genuine signature.

During the creation of a simulated forgery, the author attempts to duplicate the writing style of another individual. By doing this, the forger leaves behind little, if any, of his own distinctive writing style. By doing an emulation of someone else's signature, he also produces one of the best of all possible disguises of his own handwriting. Infrequently, some of the forger's own individual characteristics may appear in the disputed writing. The limited quantity of these characteristics which appear on those occasions is such that identification of the author almost never occurs.

If there are a sufficient number of significant differences between the questioned signature and the genuine signatures, and these same differences appear in the practiced simulations, there may be a basis to associate the forgery to the forger within some degree of probability. An absolute identification, nonetheless, even under these circumstances is infrequent.

Closely related to this form of identification process is that of determining the number of different forgers from a quantity of simulations. On occasion there will be two or more forgers attempting to reproduce the same signature. It may be possible to group or associate simulations of the same name by the combinations of defects within the forgeries. By associating and grouping the similar defects (when compared to the genuine signature) it may be possible to conclude and illustrate that there are indeed, two or more different forgers.

REASONING OF FACTS

The second documentation (exhibit 2) clearly projects the forged signature for the following reasoning

1. **Blunt starts and stops**

    In the second document it can identified that the forger places the pen point in contact with the paper, and then starts writing. When he is finished with the name or some portion thereof, he stops the pen and lifts it from the surface. This has cause the emphasized blunt start and ending where the pen was placed in contact with the surface. At times this contact is held so long that the pen contains two fluid ink in the front letter of the signature, it has wet the paper and migrate outward from the contact point.

There may be unnecessary and extraneous marks caused by pen starts and stops. The writer may decided after putting his pen in contact with the paper, that it is in the wrong spot, picks it up and moves it to a position considered more correct. Normally a signature's starts and stops are much more dynamic which can be noticed in the other two documents. The pen is moving horizontally before it contacts the paper and is lifted at the end while still in flight. This leaves a tapered appearance at the beginnings and endings of names or letters.

2. **Pen lifts and hesitation**

In this situation it can occasioned that the pen stops at an unusual point in the writing; perhaps during radical change in direction is about to take a new letter formation is about to be started. This may take on the appearance of a larger gap in the written line where one is not expected, or an overlapping of two ink lines where there should be only one continuous line which clearly in the second document but not the other two, where it seems to be following the same pattern throughout the signature .

3. **Tremor- minor shaking**

Because the creation of most forms of non-genuine signatures are little more than drawings, the pen is moving so slowly that small, sometimes microscopic changes in direction take place in what should be a fluid-looking line. The resultant line is not smooth, but reflects the "shaking" pen. It can be seen that the lines in the signature of the second documentation is much larger than the rest two and has microscopic shakes.

4. **Speed and pressure**

Again, because the pen is moving slowly rather than with the dynamic movement associated with most genuine writings, the ink line remains constant in thickness, resulting from the same constant pressure exerted on a slowly moving pen. There will be little, if any, tapering of internal lines. This is clearly evident in the second document's signature which constantly remains in the same thickness.

5. **Patching**

Sometimes when the genuine writer makes an error while writing our own signature, more commonly individuals may leave the signature alone, caring little about the mistake or imperfection, while others will simply "fix" the signature by correcting the offending portion. This might have be done this situation to make the signature more readable, or because a defect in the pen or paper has affected what we perceive to be our "normal" signature, or for some other reason that may even be subconscious.

However by analysing the previous signature that seems very unlikely. These "fixes" are patent, with no attempt made on the part of the writer to mask or otherwise hide the correction for which some letters are crossing the others out.

These signature corrections are quite different than the patching that is frequently found in non-genuine signatures. On these occasions, the writer is not attempting to make the signature more readable, but to make its appearance passable. He is fixing an obvious defect that he perceives as detectable, and might uncover his fraudulent product and foil his scheme. These usually take the form of a correction to a flaw in the writing line rather than in the form of a letter. Extensions to entry or terminal strokes, or to lower descending portions of letters, along with corrections to embellishments, are typical of non-genuine patching.

DISCUSSION

Penalty for Counterfeiting and Forgery in Canada

Each and every case of fraud is different and may result in varied consequences, however in this current scenario it is extremely vivid that the documentation was created for malicious reasoning. Therefore an individual can expect extensive prison time, as well as fines and community service work, or restitution. Other social consequences follow such as a criminal record limiting the ability to travel, and the difficulty in finding employment.

The Criminal Code of Canada states:

368(1) Uttering forged document

368(1) Every one who, knowing that a document is forged,

(a) uses, deals with or acts on it, or

(b) causes or attempts to cause any person to use, deal with or act on it, as if the document were genuine, is guilty of an indictable offence and liable to imprisonment for a term not exceeding fourteen years.

368(2) Wherever forged

368(2) For the purposes of proceedings under this section, the place where a document was forged is not material.

R.S., 1985, c. C-46, s. 368; 1992, c. 1, s. 60(F).

369 Exchequer bill paper, public seals, etc.

369 Every one who, without lawful authority or excuse, the proof of which lies on him,

(a) makes, uses or knowingly has in his possession

(i) any exchequer bill paper, revenue paper or paper that is used to make bank-notes, or

(ii) any paper that is intended to resemble paper mentioned in subparagraph (i),

(b) makes, offers or disposes of or knowingly has in his possession any plate, die, machinery, instrument or other writing or material that is adapted and intended to be used to commit forgery, or

(c) makes, reproduces or uses a public seal of Canada or of a province, or the seal of a public body or authority in Canada, or of a court of law, is guilty of an indictable offence and liable to imprisonment for a term not exceeding fourteen years. R.S., c. C-34, s. 327.

370 Counterfeit proclamation, etc.

370 Every one who knowingly

(a) prints any proclamation, order, regulation or appointment, or notice thereof, and causes it falsely to purport to have been printed by the Queen's Printer for Canada or the Queen's Printer for a province, or

(b) tenders in evidence a copy of any proclamation, order, regulation or appointment that falsely purports to have been printed by the Queen's Printer for Canada or the Queen's Printer for a province, is guilty of an indictable offence and liable to imprisonment for a term not exceeding five years. R.S., c. C-34, s. 328.

Interpretation of the Offence

Actus Reus

The act of forging the signature would be applicable enough to be considered as Actus reus for committing the act of forgery. (R v JJV, 1994 CanLII 6514 (NB CA))

Mens Rea

The mens res for forgery under s. 366(1) requires an "intent to deceive" which requires an intent that is more than mere "carelessness or negligence". The intent to deceive should generally "be coupled with an intent that the document be used to someone's prejudice, or that a person be induced to act in a certain way." Prejudice need not result as long as there was an intent for the document to be treated as genuine.(R v Benson (M.) et al., 2012 MBCA 94 (CanLII))

The Crown must show the "falsity of the endorsement the document has been shown to be a forged document and its use with knowledge is sufficient to show the commission of the offence." (R v Elkin (1978), 42 C.C.C. (2d) 185 (B.C.C.A.))

The accused must have known that "the document was false and intended for somebody to act upon it as if it was genuine.".(Sebo, [1988] A.J. No. 475 (C.A.))

It is not necessary that the accused "intended" to defraud anyone. (R v Atwal, [2015] O.J. No. 3748 (C.J.) R v G.T., 2016 CanLII 82183 (NL PC) at para 59 per Gorman PCJ)

From the situation it can be concluded that the documentation were falsely created with intent to harm the applicant

"False documents"

A fake or false item that was made as a "novelty" item cannot be a "false document" and the creation of which does not carry the requisite *mens rea* for the offence. (R v Sommani, 2007 BCCA 199 (CanLII))

The document cannot simply be "false" but it must be proven to be "false" in relation to the purpose for which it was created. (R v Benson, 2012 MBCA 94 (CanLII) ("it must be false in relation to the purpose for which it was created"))

"False document" and "forged document" are not interchangable terms. (R v Hawrish, [1986] S.J. No. 846 (C.A.))

Till the investigation now, it can be classified that the documentation was forged.

Uttering vs. Forgery

Uttering forged documents is distinct from making forged documents. The "forgery" is the making of the document, the "uttering" is the use of the document. (R v Wightman, [2003] A.J. No. 1453 (P.C.) ("Forgery deals with the making of the document; uttering deals with the use of the document."))

It could be said that the documentation was created for the misuse of it against the applicant.

CONCLUSION

It can be concluded that the documentation in (exhibit B) has a forged signature of Mr. Horace R. Carby-Samuels and with intent of malicious actions.

EXHIBIT A

Affidavit of Horace R. Carby-Samuels   Page | 5

me as well as my daughter. Marcella is in the process of completing a Ph.D and lives in Sweden. The Respondent is trying to ruin her reputation as well because he states that he wants to ensure that she will never be able to get a job or to have her name on any collegial research on which she co-operates; and he has made specious reports to her faculty in the process of promoting her expulsion from the Ph.D program. Attached as Exhibit "L" are copies of the numerous postings.

32. I truly believe that the Respondent will continue to bring frivolous actions and use the court system to continue his harassment.

33. I make this Affidavit in support of my Application to have the Respondent found to be a vexatious litigant and for no other or improper purpose.

SWORN BEFORE ME in the City
Of Ottawa, in the Province of Ontario
this 25th day of January 2017.

_____
A Commissioner, etc.

_____
Horace R. Carby-Samuels

Lauren Michelle Danaman, a Commissioner, etc.,
Province of Ontario, while Student-At-Law.
Expires June 16, 2018.

EXHIBIT B

5. With respect to the email from Maxine Fielding, I should point out that she lives in New Jersey. I sent her an email on June 1st, 2017 to inquire about Maxine's knowledge of the procedure that I was about to have, given her prior work at hospitals in the United States. Maxine replied to both myself and my daughter on June 3rd, 2017. On June 6th, Marcella communicated the care plan to Maxine in order to assure Maxine that homecare had been arranged successfully for my wife.

6. As I have mentioned in previous Affidavits, I have arranged nursing and personal care by professionals for my wife. She is not being denied access to visitors. Her relatives, friends and neighbours visit regularly without any issues. It is because of Raymond's continued attacks on both myself and my wife and his abusive behaviour towards us that has caused us to not want to see him. As a further example of his attacks, Raymond would regularly call the ambulance services to attend our home suggesting that there was an emergency. I am advised by ambulance services that they have now placed a block on his calls.

7. This recent Motion is yet a further attempt on Raymond to continually attack and abuse us. My wife is well cared for and is mentally competent. We are just tired of the constant abuse by Raymond.

8. I make this Affidavit in support of Raymond's request for an urgent Motion and for no other or improper purpose.

SWORN BEFORE ME in the City
Of Ottawa, in the Province of Ontario
this 14 day of September 2017.

_____
A Commissioner, etc.

_____
Horace R. Carby-Samuels

Zorian Adam Maksymec, a Commissioner, etc.,
Province of Ontario, while Student-At-Law.
Expires March 27, 2020.

EXHIBIT C

Affidavit of Horace R. Carby-Samuels Jr. Page | 4

22. I make this Affidavit in support of my Motion and for no other or improper purpose.

SWORN BEFORE ME in the City)
Of Ottawa, in the Province of Ontario)
this 23rd day of January 2017.)
)   *Horace R. Carby-Samuels*
)
)
_____)

A Commissioner, etc.

Lauren Michelle Deneman, a Commissioner, etc.,
Province of Ontario, while Student-At-Law.
Expires June 16, 2019.

5. With respect to the email from Maxine Fielding, I should point out that she lives in New Jersey. I sent her an email on June 1st, 2017 to inquire about Maxine's knowledge of the procedure that I was about to have, given her prior work at hospitals in the United States. Maxine replied to both myself and my daughter on June 3rd, 2017. On June 6th, Marcella communicated the care plan to Maxine in order to assure Maxine that homecare had been arranged successfully for my wife.

6. As I have mentioned in previous Affidavits, I have arranged nursing and personal care by professionals for my wife. She is not being denied access to visitors. Her relatives, friends and neighbours visit regularly without any issues. It is because of Raymond's continued attacks on both myself and my wife and his abusive behaviour towards us that has caused us to not want to see him. As a further example of his attacks, Raymond would regularly call the ambulance services to attend our home suggesting that there was an emergency. I am advised by ambulance services that they have now placed a block on his calls.

7. This recent Motion is yet a further attempt on Raymond to continually attack and abuse us. My wife is well cared for and is mentally competent. We are just tired of the constant abuse by Raymond.

8. I make this Affidavit in support of Raymond's request for an urgent Motion and for no other or improper purpose.

SWORN BEFORE ME in the City
Of Ottawa, in the Province of Ontario
this 14 day of September 2017.

Horace R. Carby-Samuels

A Commissioner, etc.

Zorian Adam Maksymec, a Commissioner, etc.,
Province of Ontario, while Student-At-Law.
Expires March 27, 2020.

Example of apparent deception

www.ingramcontent.com/pod-product-compliance
Lightning Source LLC
Chambersburg PA
CBHW052127110526
44592CB00013B/1782